THE
"MOTHER
NATURE"
SERIES

MOTHER NATURE'S
GARDEN

Pl. 1.

BUTTERCUP FLOWERS AND FRUITS (p. 31).

Mother Nature's Garden.

MOTHER NATURE'S GARDEN

HOW PLANTS LIVE
STORIES ABOUT SPECIAL PLANTS

BY

JANE LUCAS

With Four Plates in Colour
Four Half-Tone Plates and Text Illustrations

FREDERICK WARNE & CO., LTD.
LONDON AND NEW YORK

CONTENTS

INTRODUCTION

WHAT PLANTS ARE, AND HOW WE USE THEM

WHEN you talk about plants, you probably think of the flowers and vegetables in your garden, and the trees and bushes you know in woods and fields, but there are ever so many other kinds as well. There are seaweeds and mosses and toadstools and ferns, while the green scum that you find on ponds is made up of thousands of very simple little plants. The horrid little germs, which get inside you and make you ill with colds, or mumps, or measles, are plants, too, though they are so small that you cannot see them without a wonderful kind of glass called a microscope.

Some of these very tiny plants are so like the simplest kinds of animals that even very clever people cannot easily say which is which. If you have ever tried to tell anyone what is the difference between a plant and an animal, you will be surprised to find how difficult it is. They both eat and drink, and breathe and grow.

If there were no plants in the world, all the animals and human beings would die, because they would not have enough to eat, or any way of keeping themselves warm. That seems hard to believe, for when you look round your nice comfortable home, you don't see any plants at all—perhaps just a few flowers to make it look pretty.

But, if you think again, you will find that lots of your things were plants once. Some of your clothes are made of linen or cotton which are spun from plants; most of your furniture is made of wood from trees; the coal in your fire was part of a big forest thousands of years ago; the bread you eat for tea is made from wheat which grows in the fields; the jam is made of fruit and sugar (both plants, you see); the tea itself is the dried leaves of a plant, and so is the tobacco your Daddy puts in his pipe; and your big Wellington boots are made of rubber which we get from trees in hot countries.

INTRODUCTION

When you have a cold, perhaps your Mummy puts eucalyptus on your handkerchief, and rubs your chest with camphorated oil; clothes are stiffened with starch; parcels are tied with string. All these and many other things are made of plants or taken from them by clever people called chemists.

So, you see, if they are really so very useful to us, it's just as well to know a little about them. In these stories I have tried to tell you how some of them grow, and in what strange ways they look after themselves.

J.L.

PART ONE

HOW PLANTS LIVE

HOW A NEW PLANT GROWS
HOW PLANTS EAT
HOW PLANTS DRINK
HOW PLANTS TAKE CARE OF THEMSELVES
WHY PLANTS HAVE FLOWERS
THE FLOWERS' PARTY
WHY PLANTS HAVE FRUITS

HOW A NEW PLANT GROWS

WHEN you put a new seed into the ground, the first thing it needs is water, so you must remember not to sow it when the soil is hard and dry. The water which it soaks up makes it swell a good deal, and after a little while the hard, outside skin bursts, and a very small root pushes its way downwards in the ground.

Two or three thinner rootlets burst out next, and feel their way down, too, growing very slowly and gently from side to side. They creep round the stones and look for nice damp soil where they can find plenty of food.

These rootlets make the little seed quite firm in its new home, and next its skin bursts at the top, and out

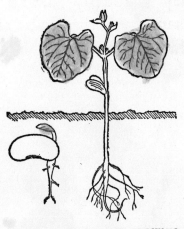

BABY BEAN PLANTS GROWING

comes the stem, wrapped up in a little sheath called a seed-leaf. The real leaves are folded neatly up inside the new shoot.

In the seed itself there is a store

Pl. 2.   A 14.

BLACKBERRY FLOWERS AND FRUITS (p. 36).
THISTLE FLOWERS READY FOR THEIR PARTY (p. 33).

Mother Nature's Garden.

of food saved up, mostly starch, and, until the new stem and root are strong enough to make fresh food, they gradually use it up, in just the same way that baby tadpoles, after they are hatched, eat up the eggs in which they grew.

The baby plant grows bigger and taller, and, if it gets plenty of sun and air, it unfolds its first leaves. When its roots find a nice rich patch of soil they fix themselves firmly in it, and grow lots of little hairs, which stretch out all round them. (You will have seen how thick and tangled they are when plants are dug up in the garden, and in the next story you will find what they are for.)

By this time, they will have used up all the food in the seed, and its empty skin will fall away. The new plant is not a baby any longer, but big enough and strong enough to find food for itself.

HOW PLANTS EAT

ALL green plants get food in two ways—part of it from the air, and part of it through their roots, down in the soil. All their drinking is done through their roots, too, so that when you give a plant water you must pour it carefully on the soil round it, and not on to the leaves.

The little root hairs, which, you remember, grow all over the roots, are really like tiny mouths for the plant; they push in among the soil, sucking up every drop of water they can find. Then they send it up the stems of the plant into the leaves as fast as possible.

Now a lot of the things which

plants like to eat are in this water, too, because the soil is full of them. Sometimes this food is very firmly mixed into the earth, and the root hairs melt it out with a kind of juice called acid. (The acid is so strong that it helps the roots to dig down into hard ground, and even into rocks. Sometimes if you find a tree which has been blown down, you will be able to see this for yourselves.) Then the melted out food is carried up the hollow stem by the water into the leaves.

But green plants also get another food from the air. It is called *carbon*. The carbon is taken into the leaves through hundreds of little mouth openings, and there, when the sun shines, it is gradually changed into sugar.

In fact, leaves are really a kind

SAP DRIPPING OUT OF A BROKEN STEM

of kitchen for the plants, where all the food is got ready for the shoots and buds and roots to use. It is carried round to them by a sweet

19

and sticky juice called sap, which will ooze out if you break a leaf stem across, so that you can easily see just what it is like.

When the plant has more food than it can use for growing, it changes it into starch, and stores it up in its root, or seeds, or different parts of its stem. (You will remember that the new baby plant feeds at first on the food which is stored up in the seed.)

Sometimes human beings, too, find these food stores good to eat. The ones we use most often are the grains of corn, which are made into flour for bread, and potatoes, which we clean and cook just as they come out of the ground.

Pl. 3.   [Photo, John J. Ward.] B 21.
THE HOLLY-TREE'S PRICKLY LEAVES (p. 26).

Mother Nature's Garden.

HOW PLANTS DRINK

THE leaves use up the food which is carried up to them, but some of the water comes out of the tiny leaf mouths all the time and is dried up by the sun and air, just as a wet towel would be if you hung it out of doors. As long as the roots go on sending up lots of water to the leaves, they keep fresh and green in spite of the sun, but sometimes things happen to stop this.

Perhaps there is no rain for a long time, and the soil gets dry and hard; or someone may dig up the roots, or cut the stems. Then the air dries all the water out of the leaves, and they wither and hang down, and very soon die. Now you can see why we put cut flowers and leaves in water, can't you? They need to drink all

A PLANT WITH AND
WITHOUT WATER

the time to prevent them from dry-ing and withering.

Plants have lots of clever ways of looking after themselves—you will read about some of them in the next story—and when the sun is specially hot for a long time, they curl up their leaves with the little mouths inside, so that they are all covered up and cannot dry so fast.

If you folded up your wet towel tightly, and then put it out of doors, it would not dry nearly so quickly, and this is what many plants do at night—they tuck all their leaves together as closely as they can, so that they will not get dry and cold. You must not think that they are asleep then, because plants do not really go to sleep, even when they close up. They are just keeping themselves warm and comfy till the sun comes back.

HOW PLANTS TAKE CARE OF THEMSELVES

YOU all know how strong and hard are the trunks and branches of big trees, and how they are only broken by really bad storms. But if you think of the flowers and climbing plants you know in the fields and how easily you can pick them, it seems wonderful that they manage to live through all kinds of weather, and that animals and insects do not harm them.

Of course, a good many of them *are* eaten, both by animals and human beings. Just think of all the fruit and vegetables that people have for dinner every day! But all the same,

HOW PLANTS TAKE CARE

lots of plants have found out how to take care of themselves and fight their enemies, so that they are left alone.

The garden Lettuce has a clever

STINGING NETTLE

way of getting rid of the ants which like to eat its thick leaves. As soon as one of them bites a small hole, the plant pours out a white, sticky juice which covers his feet and mouth and gradually hardens. Of course the ant cannot eat any more, and, if he does not manage to crawl away in time, he sticks firmly to the leaf until he dies. Then there are Stinging Nettles; not many of us like to pick them, because they are covered with little hairs which make blisters on our hands. You know, too, what prickly leaves the Holly-tree has, and how well it guards its lovely red berries. But did you ever notice that the leaves at the top of the tree often have no prickles? They are out of reach, you see, and do not need them.

Thistles have pointed spines, while Brambles and several garden berries grow thorns between their branches;

perhaps, too, you have cut your hands sometimes on the sharp leaves of some kinds of grass. All these things

WILD ROSE AND ITS HOOKED THORNS

prevent animals from eating the plants.

The thorns of the Wild Rose are shaped like hooks, and keep the long stems of the plant upright by catching on to other bushes and branches. There are many plants which cannot hold themselves up, and

SWEET PEAS AND THEIR CURLY TENDRILS

yet they manage to grow and flower quite happily. One of them is the Wild Clematis (sometimes called

A BUTTERFLY AT A FLOWER'S PARTY (p. 34).

Mother Nature's Garden.

Old Man's Beard, because of its grey, tufted fruits) which climbs all round and over the bushes and trees in the hedge-row, holding on tightly with its twisted leaf-stalks. Try to break a piece off, and you will be surprised to find how firmly it is fixed.

Other climbing plants grow little tendrils—Sweet Peas do this—or suckers, like the Virginia creeper. With these they hold themselves on to walls, poles, or fences far more firmly than we could do with our hands.

WHY PLANTS HAVE FLOWERS

WHEN you see flowers you think first about their lovely colours and shapes or perhaps their beautiful scent, but the most important things about them are tucked away inside the petals, and you probably won't notice them until the flower is withered. Do you remember in our first story we said that new plants grow from seeds? Well, the seeds are first made inside the flowers. First of all they are just little specks, each hidden away in a little green case in the middle of the flower. Before they can be real seeds, able to grow, they have to be mixed with a pretty yellow dust called *pollen*.

WHY PLANTS HAVE FLOWERS

The pollen is in the flowers, too, in smaller cases, growing on threads, and looking rather like fancy pins with yellow tops. If you look closely at the picture of a Buttercup, you will be able to see the little seed-cases and the pollen-cases growing.

Every flower has either seed-cases or pollen-cases, and some of them have both. A few manage to shake the pollen straight on to their seed-cases themselves, but most of them have to be helped, or their little seed-specks will never ripen.

The pollen is very easily shaken out of the flowers (perhaps sometimes you have had your nose dusted with it, when you have been smelling them), and so the wind helps a great deal. It blows the pollen out of its little cases in yellow clouds, and whirls it round so that lots of it is sure to fall back right on to the waiting seed-cases.

THE FLOWERS' PARTY

IN the last story you have seen two ways in which pollen can be shaken on to the seed-cases, but lots

FLOWERS OF WILD CLEMATIS SHOWING POLLEN-CASES

of flowers arrange for bees and moths and butterflies to do this for them.

It's really just as if the flowers gave the insects a party. First they store up a kind of honey in little bags under their petals—some of you have sucked sugar out of clover flowers, haven't you?—then they grow lovely party dresses for themselves — big coloured petals that the insects like to look at. Next, when the seed-specks are quite ready to be mixed with the pollen, the flowers send out the invitations. They open very wide, and give out their lovely scent.

All the insects come buzzing and fluttering up, each wanting to be first to eat the honey. They push their heads and their long tongues into the flowers down under the petals, and can you guess what happens? You remember that you get *your* nose dusted with pollen when you smell flowers? Well, so do the bees and the butterflies. They

THE FLOWERS' PARTY

get pollen on their noses and backs and feet, and the very next time they go to a flower party, it all gets rubbed off on to the seed-cases!

Now isn't that clever of the flowers?

WHY PLANTS HAVE FRUITS

AS soon as the pollen has been mixed with the seed-specks, the cases and the seeds begin to ripen, and the flower dies away, because it is not needed any more. When the seed-case is quite big, it is called the fruit of the plant—but, if you think of all the fruit you know, you will see at once that there are a great many different kinds.

Some of those which are nicest to eat, like the Apple and the Pear, are really the fat part of the flower stem, grown big, and the seed-case is right inside. Blackberries and Raspberries are made of ever so many seed-cases

Pl. 5.   C 37.

HORSE-CHESTNUT FLOWER (p. 46).

WHY PLANTS HAVE FRUITS

bunched together, one little seed in the middle of each.

But Nuts are also fruit—the kind we eat, and the big, prickly Horse-

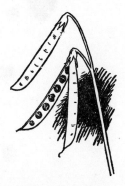

SWEET PEA PODS

chestnuts, and the little Hazel and Cobnuts in the hedges. And so are Peas and Beans, and Dandelion clocks, and all sorts of other things that don't look alike at all.

When the seed is quite ripe, it

needs to fall somehow into soft soil, so that it can grow a new little plant, like the one in our first story. It also wants to be quite away from its father and mother plant, so that it can have plenty of room for its roots. The fruit keeps the seed warm and safe until it can do this, and also helps it to move to a new home.

The fruits are moved about in several different ways. Birds peck the berries, because they are sweet and bright-coloured, and carry them about to eat, so that the seeds fall into new places.

You are sure to have told the time by a Dandelion clock, so you will know already how easily the

WHY PLANTS HAVE FRUITS

wind can blow its fruits about, because each one is fitted with a soft
tuft of greyish down. Peas, if they

DANDELION CLOCK

are left to get ripe, split open, and
the seeds spurt out. Most Nuts fall
off the trees when they are ripe, un-
less squirrels or birds carry them

39

about, and the seeds just have to wait until the hard outside shell rots away.

Poppy fruits have tiny holes round the top through which the small black seeds fall out when the wind blows them about ; prickly fruits get blown along the ground on their short bristles ; others have little hooks which catch into the fur or wool of sheep or little wild creatures, so that they get carried right away from their old homes.

I suppose sometimes you have come home from a walk with Goose-grass or Butter-burs sticking to your stockings, haven't you ? You see, although you did not know it, you were really helping them to move house !

PART TWO

STORIES ABOUT SPECIAL PLANTS

THE OAK

THOUGH all trees grow in something the same way, there are many different kinds, and if you look at them carefully when you go out for walks you will soon be able to tell one from another, even when you are quite a long way off.

Oaks have very thick, firm trunks, and long, rather downward spreading branches, which make the whole tree look wide instead of tall. The bark is very rough to see and touch, and the big roots go a long way down into the soil—you will never trip over them on the top of the ground, as you sometimes do with beech roots.

43

Oak leaves have a wavy in-and-out kind of shape which makes them quite easy to know, but the flowers are less easy to find. There are two kinds, which come out in April or May, both small and green. One is a little catkin, and holds the pollen-cases, while the other is round and has the seed-case inside.

The fruit of an Oak looks rather like an egg in an egg-cup, and is called an acorn. You are sure to have found lots of them lying about on the ground in the Autumn.

Insects are very fond of living in the bark of Oaks, and when they lay their eggs the tree grows a funny little ball round them. Some of them we call " oak-apples," though of

Pl. 6.

CUCKOO-PINT (p. 58), WOOD SORREL (p. 62).

Mother Nature's Garden.

course they are not really in the
least like fruit.

Oaks live to be very, very old—
two or three hundred years, or even
more, if they have plenty of light and
space. They do not begin to bear
fruit till they are sixty or seventy
years old. After one-hundred-and-
fifty years, they are big enough to
cut down and use for wood to make
houses and furniture. Long ago, all
our English ships were made of oak
wood, because it is the best and
strongest kind. That is why you
will sometimes find in old songs they
were called " Hearts of Oak. "

THE HORSE-CHESTNUT

NOBODY is quite sure how the Horse-chestnut got its name. It isn't really very much like a chestnut tree, and horses don't seem to eat it or take any notice of it. You will find tiny marks under the buds shaped like horse-shoes—perhaps that has something to do with it!

Like the Oak, it lives to be very old, but it grows rather faster and higher, and the wood of the trunk is not nearly so hard or so useful.

Its leaves are almost the first to open every Spring. They grow in big, brown buds, covered with a sort of sticky varnish which the sun gradually melts. Then the buds open,

THE HORSE-CHESTNUT

and out come the queer little leaves and
flower buds.   At first they are folded
up; each leaf looks like your hand
with all its finger-tips together.

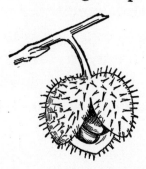

FRUIT OF HORSE-CHESTNUT

Then they slowly spread out like your
hand when it is flat on the table.

The flowers grow on lovely big
spikes, like candles on a Christmas
tree.   Usually they are white with
red and yellow dots, but some of the
smaller trees have all red flowers.

MOTHER NATURE'S GARDEN

You have probably often seen the thick, green seed-cases with their short, hard prickles, and white, milky linings. The seeds inside are shiny, reddish - brown nuts; many people call them " conkers, " and there are all sorts of jolly games you can play with them if you thread several of them together on a string.

THE HAZEL

YOU will find Hazel bushes in nearly every country hedge, but because they are cut so often, they seldom grow very big. Their leaves die away in the winter, but early in the spring Hazels grow long greenish-yellow catkins.

These " lambs' tails " are really flowers with pollen-cases inside, and if you set them swinging when they are ripe, clouds of yellow dust will blow out. The wind is always shaking them, and the pollen falls on the tiny seed-case flowers, which look like very small green buds, each with a tuft of crimson threads in the middle of it.

After this, the seed-cases in the flowers grow big and hard, until at last they turn into the small green nuts you know so well. The seeds are safe

HAZEL CATKINS (POLLEN-CASE FLOWERS)

inside, and the little dry frill which you find round the nut is what is left of the two leaflets which were once round the flower.

THE HAZEL

We cannot make anything large
or strong out of Hazel wood, but it

LEAVES AND FRUITS OF THE HAZEL

is sometimes used for walking sticks
and other small things.

A PLANT WHICH EATS
INSECTS: THE SUNDEW

SOMETIMES soil has not got as much food in it as plants need. That is the reason why few trees or bushes grow on marshy land, and those flowers that do have very small roots which spread out sideways, looking for food, instead of going downwards.

One pretty little plant that you will find in these wet and boggy places has a queer and rather cruel way of getting extra food. It is called the Sundew, and has spoon-shaped green leaves, covered with little red spikes. At the end of each spike is a drop of very sticky stuff

ACORNS: THE FRUIT OF THE OAK (p. 43).

Mother Nature's Garden.

like gum, which shines in the sunlight and is really a trap for insects. They fly or crawl on to the leaves and at once their feet and wings are smeared with the gum, so that they cannot get away.

As soon as they are caught, the leaf curls up round them, and smothers them with the gum, till they die. Then they are slowly changed into food for the plant, just as when you eat beef and potatoes your tummy changes them into the kind of stuff your body needs to make it grow. This changing is called *digestion*, and is very important.

When the insects are digested into a food juice, the leaves suck them in, and they become part of the sap. It takes two whole days for the Sundew to catch and eat an insect in this way.

The Sundew has small white flowers on long stems, but you will hardly notice them because the leaves are so bright and gay.

A PLANT WHICH WON'T
WORK: THE DODDER

ALTHOUGH most plants have to work quite hard to find and digest their food, there are a few of them who won't work properly. They like other people to take all the trouble for them.

These lazy plants are called *parasites*, and we sometimes use the same word for human beings who live by letting other people work for them. This story is about a parasite called the Dodder.

The seed falls into the ground in the ordinary way, and a very small root and a thin red shoot begin to grow, but the Dodder has no root hairs and no leaves, and there is no nice little larder of food stored up in the seed leaves, which, you remember, every baby plant unfolds first.

The stem moves backwards and forwards, looking for a plant to steal from. It grows longer and thinner, because it has no root hairs to drink with, and no leaves to eat with, so the root very soon shrivels up and dies; the long stem takes all the food away from it.

DODDER

As soon as the Dodder finds another plant—very often a young willow tree—it twists itself round and round it, and, as its root is dead and

56

useless, it is no longer fixed in the ground at all. Then it grows ever so many little suckers that make holes in the stem round which it is climbing. They steal all the food and drink from the poor willow tree which has worked so hard, and very often kill it altogether. The greedy thief then twists itself about until it finds another plant, and begins all over again.

The Dodder has a few bunchy, whitish flowers, so that it can grow new seeds, but it never needs any leaves. You see, if you steal all your food after someone else has cooked it, you don't really need a kitchen!

THE CUCKOO-PINT

THE Cuckoo-pint grows in shady hedgerows, and you are sure to have seen it if you live in the country, though you may know it by one of its other names—Wake-robin, Wild Arum, or Lords and Ladies.

When you are looking for the flowers, you will first notice a yellowish-green sheath, often spotted with purple; in the middle of this grows a dull purple spike on a thick fleshy stem. But this is only the case for the real flowers which are very tiny, and grow in a thick cluster round the bottom of the spike, carefully covered up by the sheath. In the picture, on the next page the Cuckoo-pint has been

cut in half so that you can see right
inside.

When the seed-cases are ready to

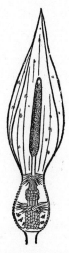

CUCKOO-PINT WITH PART OF THE SHEATH CUT
AWAY TO SHOW FLOWERS

be mixed with the pollen, the flowers
give out a rather nasty kind of scent.
This is because the visitors to their

party are some small flies who like dull colours and sour smells. They crawl in the wide opening of the sheath, down through a thick

FRUITS OF THE CUCKOO-PINT

fence of little hairs, to where the flowers are hidden—then they find that they cannot get out! The little hairs will not bend back and let them through.

60

Pl. 8.   D 60.

THE PLANT THAT EATS INSECTS:
THE SUNDEW (p. 52).

Mother Nature's Garden.

THE CUCKOO-PINT

First the flies rub their pollen off on the seed-case flowers, and sip their honey. Then the pollen-case flowers drop more pollen on to them for their next visit. As soon as this has happened, the flower petals and hairs shrivel up and die, and the little prisoners are able to fly away.

In the Autumn, you will see the fruits of the Cuckoo-pint even more easily than you found the flowers, for the sheaths are gone, and all up the fleshy spikes are lovely bright red and yellow berries.

But they are very, very poisonous to human beings, so it is best never to pick them.

THE WOOD SORREL

THE Wood Sorrel flowers in April, and, as you will guess from its name, it likes to grow under trees. It has small white flowers, and each of their five petals is faintly lined with purple. The leaves are divided into

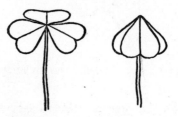

LEAVES OF WOOD SORREL OPEN AND FOLDED

three, like those of the clover, and in the day-time they are spread out wide to catch the light and air.

But at night or during rain they fold down closely against their little

THE WOOD SORREL

red stems. If you take them into a dark cupboard, they will do just the same thing. You will remember we said before that this is the way in

SEED-CASE OF WOOD SORREL (DRAWN VERY LARGE)

which plants keep themselves warm when the sun is gone.

Wood Sorrels grow a second lot of flower buds in the Summer, but the queer thing is that they never open.

They mix their pollen and seed-specks all by themselves, inside the petals, which stick together into a little cap, though the Spring flowers open quite widely.

The fruit is a little dry box, divided into two, and when the seeds are ripe, the lid part flies off. At the very same minute, the seeds are shot right out of their cases, and fall on the ground, quite a long way from their old home.

When the baby Wood Sorrel first begins to grow, its little seed leaves move very slightly all the time, so, you see, it is really rather a jumpy little plant altogether!

PRINTED FOR THE PUBLISHERS BY MACKAYS LTD. CHATHAM

41/10/35